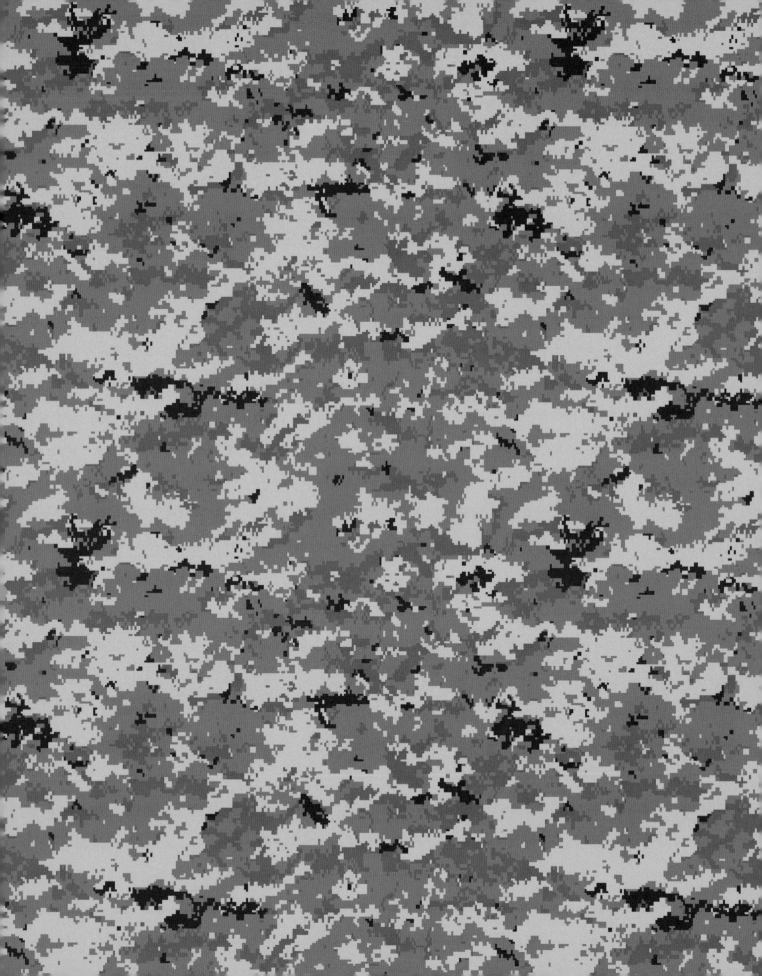

U.S. SPECIAL FORCES

DELTA FORCE

JIM WHITING

CREATIVE ● EDUCATION

PUBLISHED BY Creative Education

P.O. Box 227, Mankato, Minnesota 56002

Creative Education is an imprint of The Creative Company

www.thecreativecompany.us

DESIGN AND PRODUCTION BY Christine Vanderbeek

ART DIRECTION BY Rita Marshall

PRINTED IN the United States of America

PHOTOGRAPHS BY

Alamy (AF Archive, Aurora Photos, peter jordan, Moviestore collection
Ltd, Ivan Nesterov, PF-[MIL], United Archives GmbH, US Air Force
Photo, US Army Photo, ZUMA Press, Inc.), Corbis (AP, Bettmann,
CORBIS, Ashley Gilbertson/VII, Ed Kashi/VII, FRANCIS SPECKER/AP,
Sygma, Zuma Press/ZUMA), Getty Images (Ulrich Baumgarten,
Monty Brinton/CBS, Greg Mathieson/Mai/Mai/Time Life Pictures,
WIN MCNAMEE/AFP), iStockphoto (sadikgulec, spxChrome),
Shutterstock (ALMAGAMI, Condor 36, gst)

LIBRARY OF CONGRESS CATALOGING-IN-PUBLICATION DATA

Whiting, Jim.

Delta Force / Jim Whiting.

p. cm. — (U.S. Special Forces)

Includes bibliographical references and index.

Summary: A chronological account of the American military special
forces unit known as Delta Force, including key details about
important figures, landmark missions, and controversies.

ISBN 978-1-60818-461-3

1. United States. Army. Delta Force—History—Juvenile literature.

I. Title.

UA34.S64W448 2014

356'.167—dc23 2013036170

CCSS: RI.5.1, 2, 3, 8; RH.6-8.4, 5, 6, 8

FIRST EDITION

9 8 7 6 5 4 3 2 1

TABLE OF CONTENTS

★ ★ ★

Members of the German special operations unit GSG-9 function as part of the federal police.

FORCE FACTS Delta Force often cross-trains with similar units from other countries, such as Britain's SAS, Germany's GSG-9, and France's GIGN.

U.S. SPECIAL FORCES

INTRODUCTION

SIX WEEKS AFTER THE INVASION OF IRAQ ON MARCH 19, 2003, United States president George W. Bush announced that the mission to overthrow Saddam Hussein had been accomplished. The next step was to locate the *deposed* dictator, who had disappeared as his armies crumbled around him. In July that year, his two sons were killed. But their father's whereabouts remained a mystery.

It seemed likely that Hussein was hiding near his birthplace of Tikrit. A task force consisting of Delta Force operators and other special forces made at least a dozen raids on suspected locations in the next six months without success. On December 13, they captured a man with close ties to Hussein and learned enough to believe that they were close to his location. That evening they raided a farmhouse, capturing two men. One was Hussein's personal cook.

The operators combed the area around the farmhouse, though there was no sign of the tunnels in which Hussein was reportedly hiding. They were about to move away and search a larger area when one man saw something suspicious through his night-vision goggles. The bricks and dirt at his feet were arrayed too neatly. A piece of thread protruded from the ground. Quickly, two dozen fellow operators joined him. They scraped away the dirt and saw a plug. Weapons at the ready, they pulled up the plug. Beneath it was a man with a long, scraggly beard.

"I am Saddam Hussein," the man said. "I am the president of Iraq, and I am willing to negotiate."

After the terrorist attacks in 2001, George W. Bush committed the military to discovering the source.

U.S. SPECIAL FORCES

DISASTER IN THE DESERT

COLONEL CHARLES BECKWITH WAS A FRUSTRATED MAN. A member of Army Special Forces (a force more popularly known as the Green Berets), he served a ***tour of duty*** in the early 1960s with the British Special Air Service (SAS), the world's most highly regarded antiterrorist unit. The primary focus of the Green Berets was helping to train the troops of U.S. allies under attack by other countries. However, Beckwith believed that "the American Army not only needed a Special Forces capability, but an SAS one; not only a force of teachers, but of doers." There was no question that Beckwith was a "doer." Nicknamed "Chargin' Charlie" for his hard-driving attitude and willingness to engage the enemy, Beckwith repeatedly urged the formation of an American unit similar to SAS. But his pleas fell on deaf ears.

Starting with the massacre of 11 members of the Israeli team at the 1972 Summer Olympics in Munich, Germany, a wave of terrorism swept through the world. Several governments established elite units similar to SAS to combat the emerging threat. In 1977, the German group known as GSG-9 freed hostages from a hijacked airliner that had landed in Somalia. An impressed U.S. president Jimmy Carter asked his *Joint Chiefs of Staff* if the U.S. military had a similar unit. No, he was told. Army vice chief of staff General Edward Meyer then threw his support behind

In 1977, Germany's GSG-9 unit rescued all 86 passengers aboard the hijacked Lufthansa Flight 181.

Beckwith. In November 1977, Beckwith became commanding officer of the newly formed 1st Special Forces Operational Detachment-Delta (SFOD-D), otherwise known as Delta Force. He was given 18 months to establish a highly motivated, highly skilled unit of 100 men. Nearly 200 men began the training at the Fort Bragg, North Carolina, headquarters, but considerably less than half of them completed the process.

In late October 1979, it was time to see how well the operators had learned their lessons. They faced a simulated hostage rescue situation involving a hijacked airliner. The exercise generated so much noise that the county sheriff filed a complaint the following morning. Each person playing the role of terrorist was "shot" twice in the forehead—wounds that, in reality, would become a Delta Force "signature." On November 4, the trainees faced an exercise involving two groups of hostages: one on the airplane and the other in the airport terminal building. The rescue missions had to be simultaneous. While the assault on the aircraft began precisely when it was supposed to, the one on the terminal was delayed by 45 seconds. In real life, that glitch could have proved fatal for the hostages and/or operators. Nevertheless, those who were assigned to judge the new group's readiness—from the U.S. military and elite foreign antiterrorist units—decided that Delta was fully combat-ready.

Beckwith and his officers celebrated their success, and then went to bed well after midnight. A few short hours later, they were awakened with the news that a mob of Iranians had stormed the U.S. embassy in Tehran. Several dozen blindfolded American citizens were photographed being paraded through the embassy grounds. While diplomatic efforts to free the hostages began immediately, so did planning for a possible *covert* rescue. It was clear that this was precisely the kind of mission for which Delta Force had been created.

Based on his unit's performance in the just-concluded

While serving in Vietnam, "Chargin' Charlie" Beckwith was nearly killed by a bullet to the stomach.

exercises, Beckwith believed that storming the embassy compound and rescuing the hostages was feasible. But the primary challenge lay in getting Beckwith and his men into Iran to launch the assault. Then there would be the matter of *exfiltrating* them with all the hostages. Absolute secrecy was critical. If the Iranians got the slightest whiff of a rescue operation, they might execute the hostages or move them to a secret location where a rescue would be impossible.

According to plan, six Hercules C-130 transport aircraft would carry the men, their equipment, and fuel to a remote part of the Iranian desert codenamed Desert One. There they would meet eight navy RH-53D Sea Stallion helicopters from the aircraft carrier USS *Nimitz*. The helicopters would fly the men to a hideout near Tehran. From there, Delta Force operators would drive trucks to the embassy and launch the assault. When it was over, the helicopters would pick up everyone and return to Desert One. The C-130s would fly them to safety, and the choppers would return to the *Nimitz*. Because of the distance between the ship and the landing site and the necessity for the operation to take place under cover of darkness, two nights would be required. The first night would end with all the aircraft concealed beneath camouflage netting, in preparation for the rescue the following night.

Aided by a steady stream of *intelligence*, Delta Force rehearsed Operation Eagle Claw until it began on April 24, 1980. The mission seemed doomed from the beginning. Two of the eight Sea Stallions—which had a long history of mechanical problems—malfunctioned on the way in. After the six others arrived at Desert One by as much as an hour and a half late, a third helicopter became inoperable. Because mission rules required a

Situated between Iraq and Afghanistan, Iran was on the brink of revolution in 1977.

minimum of six helicopters to be used, Beckwith had to call off the assault.

Meanwhile, none of the aircrafts' engines had been turned off, so for three hours, the engines had churned up clouds of sand and dust that significantly obscured vision. As one of the helicopters took off for the return flight, it accidentally flew into a fuel-laden transport. The collision began a fire that incinerated eight men in the two aircraft and cooked off ammunition. The resulting explosions showered the area with deadly shrapnel. Miraculously, there were no further fatalities. Beckwith ordered everyone onto the C-130s. The helicopters, full of mission details, were left behind and captured by the Iranians.

Eagle Claw had become a fiasco, and the national embarrassment that followed is probably one of the reasons why Ronald Reagan defeated President Carter in the election that November. The failure claimed another casualty. Many people, especially in the media, blamed Beckwith. He left the military in 1981 and formed his own private security company, which he named SAS of Texas.

Captain John R. Batzler (left) commanded the USS Nimitz *during Operation Eagle Claw.*

Before leaving military service, however, Beckwith analyzed the operation's failure for a congressional committee. Among the many reasons for its downfall, he said, was that there hadn't been enough coordination among the services. In particular, the helicopter pilots had tried as hard as they could but lacked the necessary training to fly such a difficult and challenging mission. "My recommendation," he said, "is to put together an organization that contains everything it will ever need, an organization that would include Delta, the Rangers, the Navy SEALs, Air Force pilots, its own staff, its own support people, its own aircraft and helicopters. Make this organization a permanent military unit. Allocate sufficient funds. And give it sufficient time to recruit, assess, and train its people."

Congress and the U.S. military agreed. The result was the formation in 1987 of the U.S. Special Operations Command (SOCOM), which oversees all special forces operations. It has its own command structure, operates independently of the individual services, and reports directly to the Joint Chiefs of Staff. Delta Force is a key element of SOCOM. While many SOCOM missions are shrouded in secrecy, this is especially true of Delta—the U.S. government won't officially acknowledge that the unit even exists.

Iranians displayed a helicopter from Eagle Claw as a reminder of American failure.

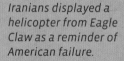

FORCE FACTS An anonymous operator compared Eagle Claw with a famous American battle: "The difference between this and the Alamo is that Davy Crockett didn't have to fight his way in."

ONLY THE TOUGHEST MAKE THE GRADE

U.S. SPECIAL FORCES

MOST SPECIAL FORCES PROVIDE DESCRIPTIONS OF THE REquirements to join the force that are readily available. In some cases, such as with the Air Force Special Operations Command (AFSOC), entry into programs such as pararescue and special operations weather is open to those with no previous military experience who can pass rigorous physical, psychological, and mental tests.

There is no official site that provides details about becoming a member of Delta Force. However, one thing is certain. No one comes in "off the street" and is whisked off to Delta Force training. Rather, becoming eligible to join what is often called "the Unit" involves perhaps the most demanding selection process in the entire military.

It's believed that Delta Force actively seeks recruits. Notices posted at army bases throughout the country and overseas draw many applicants. Word of mouth and personal recommendations account for others. It seems likely that most of the respondents come from within the army, primarily from the Green Berets and the Rangers. Other candidates come from the Army Reserves, the National Guard, and even a smattering from other branches of the armed forces. Prospective Delta Force officers must be captains or majors in rank, with at least 12 months of successful command experience under their belts. *Enlisted men* must be sergeants with a minimum of four years of service and at least two years remaining.

Recruiters emphasize the dangers of becoming part of the Unit. Eric Haney, one of the original members of Delta Force,

U.S. special forces snipers must train to operate in all kinds of conditions and terrain.

FORCE FACTS Sometimes Delta Force personnel wear uniforms, but the uniforms have no standard markings such as name, rank, or branch of the service.

notes that a 1982 picture showed a group of the men. "In the course of the next decade, nearly every man in that photo would be wounded at least once, some multiple times," he noted. "A number would be killed in action." Despite the risks, a Delta Force officer identified by the *pseudonym* Dalton Fury explains the attraction: "Many red-blooded American men want to be special operators, just as many young boys want to be professional ball players, because it is arguably the highest achievement in the military profession."

Prospective operators begin with the three- to four-week Selection and Assessment course. The program starts off with physical exams that demonstrate the candidates' fitness for both high-altitude parachuting and scuba diving, followed by a qualifying test consisting of six activities: the inverted crawl (in which the men lie on their backs, raise their rear ends, then scuttle forward using their elbows and feet for motive power); pushups; sit-ups; a 2-mile (3.2 km) run; a 100-meter swim wearing *fatigues* and combat boots; and an obstacle course called run, dodge, and jump. The next level is considerably more difficult to pass, as it includes an 18-mile (29 km) road march with heavy pack, followed by a battery of mental and psychological tests.

Then comes the truly hard part. Contrary to popular belief, Delta Force operators don't always go in with guns blazing. Sometimes knowing not to shoot is as important as knowing when to do so. But when a clear opportunity presents itself, the operators must take advantage. During the 1972 Olympics hostage crisis, two German sharpshooters—who were fully qualified in their specialty as a result of their skill and training—had clear shots at the terrorists. But they didn't fire.

According to Beckwith, those sharpshooters lacked resolve and failed to function under conditions of severe stress. In order to identify candidates who wouldn't falter in adverse conditions, he adapted a selection method from SAS. Each day in

Special operations training assessments push recruits to their physical and mental limits.

FORCE FACTS Delta Force's original headquarters at Fort Bragg was the prison stockade, which had recently been closed and the inmates transferred to other bases.

the final stage of training, prospective operators face a series of land navigation tests in mountainous terrain. They start with a distance of 6.2 miles (10 km), and both the distance and the amount of weight carried in their *rucksacks* go up daily. The men also have to meet time requirements as they travel from point to point, but they are not told what those targets are. Racing against an unknown clock is meant to induce stress.

The sheer physical demands experienced near the final march are also stress-inducing. With no recovery days for the duration of the test, the men are exhausted and tempted to drop out by the time they face the final day: 40 miles (74 km) in 20 hours. As Beckwith observes, "It was then, after the twelfth hour, that many men quit, or rested too long, or slowed to a pace that prohibited them from meeting the time requirement. A few others had the sense of purpose, the courage, the will, the guts to reach down inside themselves for that intangible trait that enabled them to carry on."

The process is purposely designed to weed out most of the candidates, and it succeeds. In Haney's group, for example, only 18 of the original 163 men survived. And soon after all the marching is over, there are further hurdles that must be cleared in the form of questionnaires, yet another psychological exam, and a grilling by the Commanders' Board—a group consisting of the Unit's overall commander, the command sergeant major (the highest-ranking enlisted man), and a dozen or so other officers and enlisted men. In Haney's group, six more failed. Final tally: 12 of 163, or 7 percent. This figure is fairly typical of each new group of selectees.

The handful of men who pass Selection and Assessment move on to the six-month-long Operator Training Course (OTC). According

Military spokespeople refuse to comment on Delta Force's presence at Fort Bragg.

Fort Bragg
Home Of
The Airborne
And
Special Operations Forces

to reports, the training compound—located in a remote part of the sprawling Fort Bragg grounds—includes several state-of-the-art shooting facilities, an Olympic-sized swimming pool, a dive tank, a three-story climbing wall, and more. The basic and single most essential skill is marksmanship, and practicing that involves a lot of shooting. Because Delta Force often uses weapons that differ from the other service branches, mastering them can involve a steep learning curve. According to reports, the men need to be 100 percent accurate in shooting at targets up to 600 yards (550 m) away and 90 percent for distances of up to 1,000 yards (915 m).

Many of the situations operators face in the field involve close quarters combat (CQC). To develop proficiency in CQC, trainees spend considerable amounts of time in a *shoot house*. Silhouettes representing either terrorists or hostages pop up at rapid intervals. Shooters must make instantaneous decisions about identifying them and act accordingly. "There's no more than seven seconds between entering a room and clearing it before things go sour," Beckwith said.

Fort Bragg allows special operations units to practice large-scale staged firefights.

Other aspects of training include working with explosives (both existing and *improvised*), breaching doors and entering buildings, hand-to-hand combat, high-altitude parachute jumping, and scuba diving. As Haney explains, "in order to become experts at counterterrorism, we had to first become terrorists."

One thing Delta Force personnel don't have to worry about is maintaining their uniforms. They are given wide latitude in their dress and appearance. Many operatives have beards and long hair, and they wear grungy civilian clothing. The object is to look as little like soldiers as possible.

The organization of Delta closely mimics that of SAS. There are three combat squadrons known simply as A, B, and C. Each squadron has two or three sub-squadrons, which consist of one sniper troop plus one or two assault troops. In turn, each troop has four or five 4-man teams. While many regular army units are also based on this small-team concept, their training allows them to operate independently only for short periods of time. Delta Force teams, on the other hand, can easily operate on their own for much longer periods.

These 3 squadrons reportedly contribute about 250 "boots on the ground." They form the tip of the Delta Force spear and are the ones who are involved in direct action. According to estimates, there are another 750 members of Delta Force. These include specialists in mechanics, communications, intelligence-gathering, and other support functions. Haney notes, "operators always knew that we were backed up and supported by the absolute masters of their professions, no matter what their specialty—parachute riggers, administrative or finance clerks, cooks, supply personnel, communications specialists, or gunsmiths." There are rumors that a handful of women are part of the intelligence-gathering arm. If those rumors are true, such operatives are the only females in Delta Force.

Breaching involves forcing open doors using explosives, ballistics, or other means.

FORCE FACTS Operators must become proficient at shooting while lying on the ground, standing, and kneeling as well as while walking and even running.

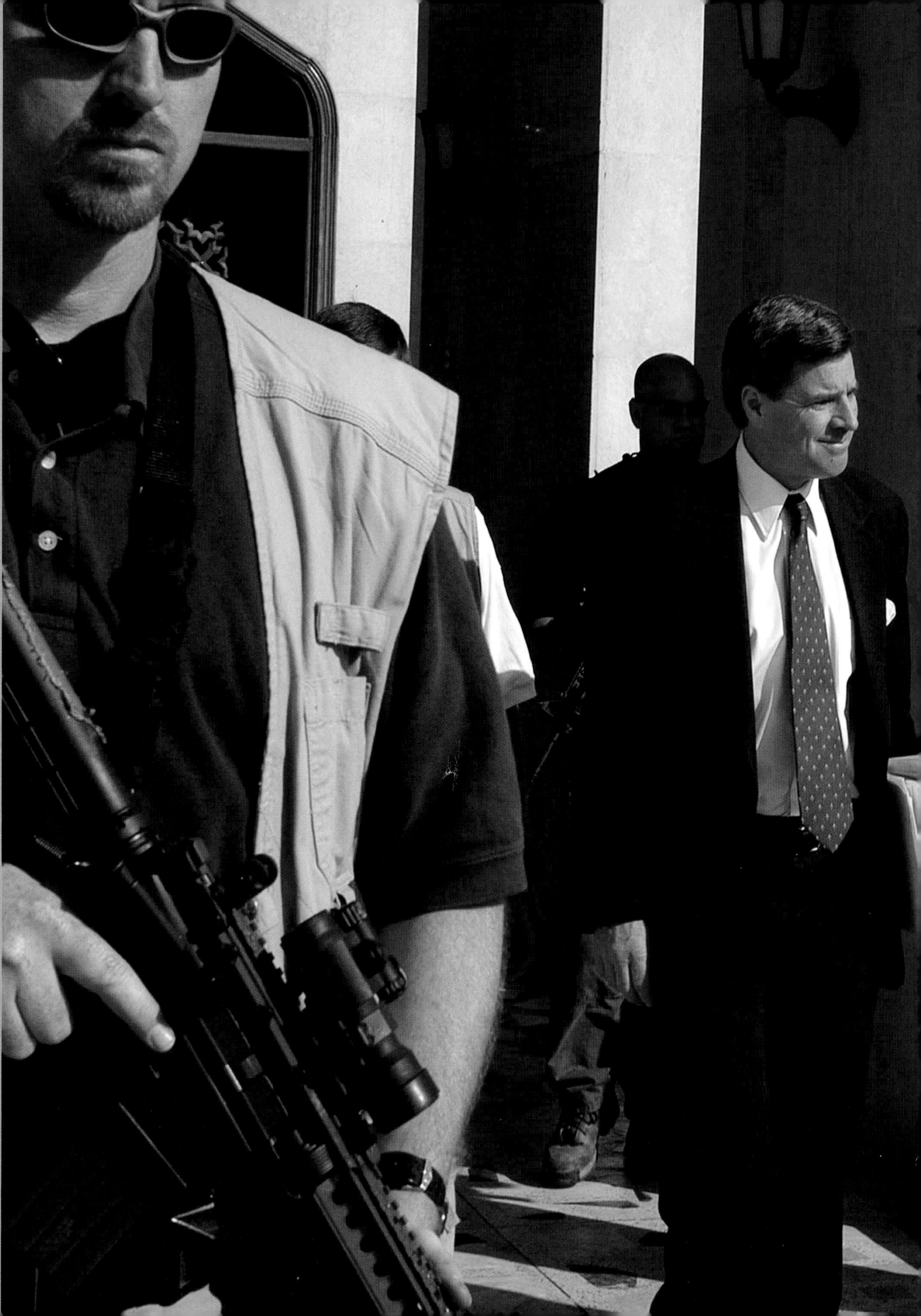

A GLOBAL REACH IN FACT AND FICTION

FROM DELTA FORCE'S HOME BASE AT FORT BRAGG, OPERAtors can be dispatched to virtually any hot spot on the globe. Reported operations have taken place in Central and South America, Africa, Europe, Southeast Asia, and—especially in recent years—the Middle East, in particular the countries of Afghanistan and Iraq.

Discussions about Delta Force may result in comparisons with the U.S. Navy's SEALs, who received a great deal of favorable publicity for taking down 9/11 terrorist mastermind Osama bin Laden in 2011. Retired army Colonel Ken Allard tried to put the two groups into perspective. "Silence is security," he observed. "They can get more done the quieter they do things. Ever since Delta Force was created, they have been the quintessential [definitive] shadow forces. That's not going to change, even with the recent publicity about the SEALs.... SEALs like to be seen. They have a great PR [public relations] machine. Delta, on the other hand, are very quiet and reserved by comparison. They embrace a culture of secrecy more so than the Navy."

In addition to the types of direct action for which Delta Force is most famous, another area of their expertise is executive protection. Photographs of high-ranking military officers or diplomats arriving at a destination often show several nearby men wearing civilian clothing and dark glasses, looking about warily, and brandishing automatic weapons. To further conceal their identity and maintain secrecy, a black rectangle is placed over the men's faces in nearly all such photos.

To carry out its missions, the primary weapon of Delta Force

Top U.S. officials working in Iraq, such as diplomat Paul Bremer III, required elite and continuous protection.

operators is the HK416 assault rifle, which is used in place of the Colt M4A1 that is standard with most other American special forces. The HK416 is the result of a close collaboration between Delta Force and the noted German arms manufacturer Heckler and Koch. The weapon comes in 4 barrel lengths, ranging from just more than 10 to 20 inches (25.4–50.8 cm). Weighing less than 7 pounds (3.2 kg) without accessories, it fires 10 to 15 rounds per second and is accurate out to a quarter of a mile (400 m). Like most other guns of its type, it is equipped with slots and brackets on the barrel that allow a variety of accessories—such as aiming devices, lighting systems, a 40-millimeter grenade launcher, a *foregrip*, and numerous others—to be attached to and removed from the weapon in a matter of seconds. Most operators also carry a pistol, such as the Colt 1911A1—one of the most successful and long-lasting firearms ever produced—or, especially in desert conditions because of its better resistance to sand, the Glock 22, a .40 caliber *polymer* handgun.

Delta Force personnel can call upon an assortment of secondary armament as well: shotguns, *squad automatic weapons*, light and heavy machine guns, sniper rifles, grenade launchers, and still others. They have access to some of the best gunsmiths in the entire military, who customize the weapons to fit the operators' individual needs. These gunsmiths make slight adjustments to the guns' moving parts, sights, grips, and so forth—which can often make the difference in life-and-death situations—and prepare handcrafted sniper ammunition.

In addition to its vast weapons arsenal, Delta Force reportedly has the services of its own aviation platoon. This group includes as many as a dozen helicopters that are outfitted to appear as if they are civilian aircraft. Operators may also team up with the "Night Stalkers," the elite 160th Special Operations Airborne Regiment (SOAR). The Night Stalkers specialize in flying helicopters carrying special forces troops into enemy territory

Timing of transportation and extraction is of the essence during any Delta Force mission.

and back out again.

Because of the *mystique* that surrounds Delta Force, it has been featured in a variety of media. As Dalton Fury observes, "Delta operators are intuitively winners, and although many folks openly cheer for the underdog, we secretly prefer being with the winners."

Delta Force is a staple element of many military adventure novels. One of the most notable is Stephen Hunter's *The Day before Midnight* (1989). Terrorists are seeking the launch codes for a nuclear missile, and Delta Force must stop them. The task is especially difficult because the terrorists are Russian special forces troops, making them especially formidable adversaries. And the Delta Force leader, Dick Puller, is modeled on Charlie Beckwith. Several nonfiction books about Delta Force have also been published, starting with Beckwith's *Delta Force* (first published in 1983, then reissued with an epilogue in 2000), which offers detailed descriptions of the Unit's founding and the Eagle Claw mission.

Fury commanded a Delta Force group that came very close to capturing or killing Osama bin Laden in 2001. Seven years later he published *Kill bin Laden*, which describes both the actual mission as well as his experiences in training. Fury has also written a series of Delta Force novels, the first two of which are *Black Site* (2011) and *Tier One Wild* (2012). The authoritative publishing industry magazine *Publishers Weekly* called *Black Site* "a thriller that crackles with gut-wrenching action and authenticity."

On television, 24 was one of the highest-rated shows during its eight-season run. The main character of Jack Bauer (played by actor Kiefer Sutherland) was a former Delta Force operator who uses his skills to his advantage against the bad guys. Delta Force also played a central role in the series' third season,

Episodes of 24 are structured in real time to mimic the stress of real-life operations.

with one of its elements helping Bauer track down terrorists who have a deadly virus. Although the final season was in 2010, 24's ongoing popularity has spawned a movie that is likely to be released in 2014 or 2015. Another TV series, *The Unit*, was about Delta Force operators' experiences in the field and their home lives. It aired for four seasons and featured Eric Haney as co-creator, technical adviser, and co-producer. He also served as a technical adviser for the 2004 movie *Spartan*, whose opening scenes display the Delta Force selection process.

Four major motion pictures have been devoted entirely to Delta Force. The first was *The Delta Force* (1986), featuring long-time movie star Lee Marvin and action hero Chuck Norris. The plot was based on the real-life 1985 hijacking of an American airliner in the Middle East by a group of terrorists who took the passengers hostage and held them at gunpoint. The film gains authenticity by using several incidents from the actual hijacking, such as the execution of a U.S. Navy diver. The ending,

Before acting, Chuck Norris served in the U.S. Air Force and gained fame as a martial artist.

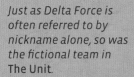
however, was different. In the film, Delta Force rescues the passengers and takes down the terrorists. In real life, Delta Force was prevented from carrying out a rescue mission when Algeria wouldn't allow the men to use their country as a staging area. Neither of the two sequels—*Delta Force 2: The Colombian Connection* (1990) and *Delta Force 3: The Killing Game* (1991)— did as well at the box office as the original, nor did reviewers think much of them.

The fourth Delta Force-specific film is 2001's *Black Hawk Down*, based on the Unit's involvement in the disastrous Battle of Mogadishu eight years earlier. The movie closely follows events described in the best-selling 1999 book of the same name by Mark Bowden. What was designed to be a fairly routine operation—a force consisting of Delta operators, a unit of Army Rangers, and a few Navy SEALs snapping up associates of a notorious warlord in Mogadishu, the capital of Somalia—quickly became a desperate battle for survival. The men found themselves surrounded by thousands of armed Somalis in what some people called the most intense firefight experienced by American military personnel since the Vietnam War. Most reviewers liked the film, and *Newsweek* magazine's Evan Thomas—author of several books on military themes—wrote, "Though [*Black Hawk Down*] depicted a shameful defeat, the soldiers were heroes willing to die for their brothers in arms. The movie showed brutal scenes of killing, but also courage, stoicism, and honor."

Just as Delta Force is often referred to by nickname alone, so was the fictional team in The Unit.

FORCE FACTS *The Unit* star Dennis Haysbert played the first fictional African American president in *24* and believed his success in that role helped to pave the way for the 2008 election of Barack Obama to the American presidency.

CLASSIFIED INFORMATION

U.S. SPECIAL FORCES

Nearly all of Delta Force's missions remain classified. Media accounts of successful operations conducted by Delta Force are often credited in generalized terms to "coalition forces," "American special operation forces," and "U.S. commandos." Their missions may also be attributed to other countries—or simply not mentioned at all.

A few have been made public. Unfortunately, this relative handful includes three of the best-known special forces failures—Operation Eagle Claw, Mogadishu, and the narrow escape of Osama bin Laden in 2001—all of which are closely associated with Delta Force. In the eyes of many knowledgeable observers, this affiliation does a grave disservice to the Unit's reputation.

For example, there is a strong belief that Beckwith was unfairly made the *scapegoat* when Operation Eagle Claw broke down and became a *propaganda* triumph for Iran. Danny Coulson founded the Federal Bureau of Investigation's elite Hostage Rescue Team (HRT), the country's primary domestic counterterrorism unit, modeling it after Delta Force and using many of the same training methods. As he explains, "If a bus hauling the Denver Broncos to the Super Bowl crashed, we wouldn't say the team lost the game. I thought it grossly unfair that the affair tarnished Delta's public image ... Delta was, and is, known for its superb planning process, its scientific approach to assaults, and its extraordinary marksmanship and physical training. It is equal or superior to any other counterterror force in the world."

Because of *Black Hawk Down*—both the film and the book—the Battle of Mogadishu became especially well known.

After a decade of eluding capture, Osama bin Laden was killed in 2011 by U.S. SEAL Team Six.

FORCE FACTS The actors who played Delta Force operators in the film *Black Hawk Down* underwent two weeks of intensive military-style training at Fort Bragg.

According to the operational plan—which should have lasted an estimated 90 minutes—American troops would quickly seize the building where their targets were meeting and return to base with their captives. But they met unexpected resistance, and then two Black Hawk helicopters were shot down. The Americans soon found themselves surrounded. Two Delta Force operators—Master Sergeant Gary Gordon and Sergeant First Class Randy Shughart—were later awarded the Medal of Honor. They volunteered to go to the aid of the crew of a downed helicopter but were overrun and killed after inflicting heavy casualties. The remaining besieged men were finally rescued 17 hours later by a combined force of Malaysians, Pakistanis, and the U.S. 10th Mountain Division. Eighteen Americans were killed and more than 70 were wounded. The nation was horrified by televised images of gleeful Somalis dragging the battered corpses of dead Americans through the streets of Mogadishu. Not long afterward, president Bill Clinton withdrew all American forces from Somalia.

Yet as *Black Hawk Down* author Mark Bowden points out, "Nothing can diminish the professionalism and dedication of the Rangers and Special Forces units who fought there that day.... it was in large part the men of Delta Force and the SEALs who held things together and got most of the force out alive." And the website of the authoritative Special Operations Forces Situation Report (SOFREP) observes, "Describing Delta's actions in the Battle of Mogadishu as a failure is even more at odds with the reality on the ground. Mark Bowden's in-depth account, *Black Hawk Down*, depicted the Unit's operators as awe-inspiring soldiers whose technical proficiency, training, and courage under fire went a long way toward preventing what otherwise might have been a far more catastrophic result. Master Sergeant Paul Howe, a former Delta operator who took part in the fight, considered it a most decisive victory for the United States, calling it

Critics have accused Black Hawk Down *of inaccurately portraying real-life soldiers and Somalis.*

'one of the most one-sided battles in American history.'"

Eight years later, Delta Force seemed on the verge of capturing al Qaeda leader Osama bin Laden just a few months after 9/11. Aided by other American special forces—particularly Air Force Special Operations Command combat controllers who called in punishing air strikes—Afghan militia had pushed bin Laden into the Tora Bora mountains of eastern Afghanistan. A small group of special forces—some 40 Delta Force operators and a handful of Green Berets and British commandos under the overall command of Dalton Fury—began closing in. Fury requested the assistance of a unit of Army Rangers to seal off potential escape routes, but the request was denied by higher military authorities for reasons that remain controversial. Fury believes that his men were less than 1.2 miles (1.9 km) from their quarry, or target.

They got no closer. Bin Laden escaped, and many people believe that his escape added to the almost mystical regard in which he was held by his followers. "The *Monday-morning quarterbacks* portrayed a military blunder and cried mission failure," Fury says. "Even the most seasoned operator, our squadron sergeant major, said to me before we left the battlefield, in true realist fashion, 'Sir, what was the mission? We failed!'"

Among other crimes, Saddam Hussein's regime carried out torture and mass killings of citizens.

Fury believes otherwise. "We went into a hellish land that was considered impregnable and controlled by al Qaeda fighters who had helped defeat the Soviet Union on that same turf," he wrote. "And we heard the demoralized Osama bin Laden speak on the radio, pleading for women and children to fight for him. Then he abandoned them all and ran from the battlefield." CNN national security analyst Peter Bergen blamed U.S. army chief General Tommy Franks for not deploying the

Rangers, calling it "one of the greatest military blunders in recent U.S. history" and thereby helping to provide the impetus
for the War in Afghanistan.

However, when it came to locating Saddam Hussein and his
sons Uday and Qusay, the Unit was a perfect three-for-three.
Like Saddam himself and many of his close associates, the sons
had disappeared as coalition troops closed in. Acting on a tip,
Delta Force and units of the 101st Airborne Division surrounded
a fortified house in Mosul, Iraq, on July 22, 2003. Uday and Qusay
Hussein, along with a bodyguard and Qusay's 14-year-old son,
were holed up inside and refused to surrender peaceably. To pro-
tect the operators, anti-tank missiles and helicopter-mounted
heavy machine guns raked the house. As they advanced into the
structure, operators found that Qusay and the bodyguard were
dead. A Delta operator found Uday wounded but still capable
of firing and shot him twice in defense. Qusay's son had taken
shelter under a bed and was still firing his automatic weapon.

*The Mosul villa was
severely damaged after
U.S. troops stormed it
to take out the fugitive
Hussein brothers.*

Operators had no choice but to take him out.

While Delta Force is primarily associated with operations in which they shoot to kill, one episode reveals what their training and expertise can accomplish without loss of life. In 2004, four Italians and a Pole were kidnapped in the Iraqi capital of Baghdad. One of the Italians was executed soon afterward, and the others vanished. Two months later, American forces received credible intelligence about the captives' location—and their likely imminent execution. Several days of covert surveillance of the suspected site and eavesdropping on the kidnappers' cell phones revealed the captors' customary habits, allowing a rescue plan to be developed. On the day of the rescue, helicopters packed with operators approached the kidnappers' hiding place at high speed, and then tipped up their noses at the last moment to halt the crafts' momentum. The men scrambled out of the choppers and burst inside the building. The speed with which the operation was conducted caught the kidnappers completely unprepared, and they quickly surrendered. The hostages were hungry and frightened but otherwise unharmed.

The quote, "People sleep peaceably in their beds at night only because rough men stand ready to do violence on their behalf" is often attributed to George Orwell, the British author of such books as *Animal Farm*. Whether he said it or not, there can be little doubt that it is a perfect description of Delta Force and its role in today's often-violent world.

In 2005, Delta Force rescued Susan Hallums's ex-husband, Roy, held hostage by Iraqi kidnappers for 10 months.

FORCE FACTS To help preserve the secrecy of Delta Force, its personnel files are removed from regular army records and maintained by the secret Department of the Army Security Roster.

From 2010 to 2012, East Africans fled to refugee camps during a drought-induced famine.

FORCE FACTS Delta Force was in Somalia as part of a U.S. humanitarian program in the wake of a devastating famine that had killed more than 300,000 people in that country.

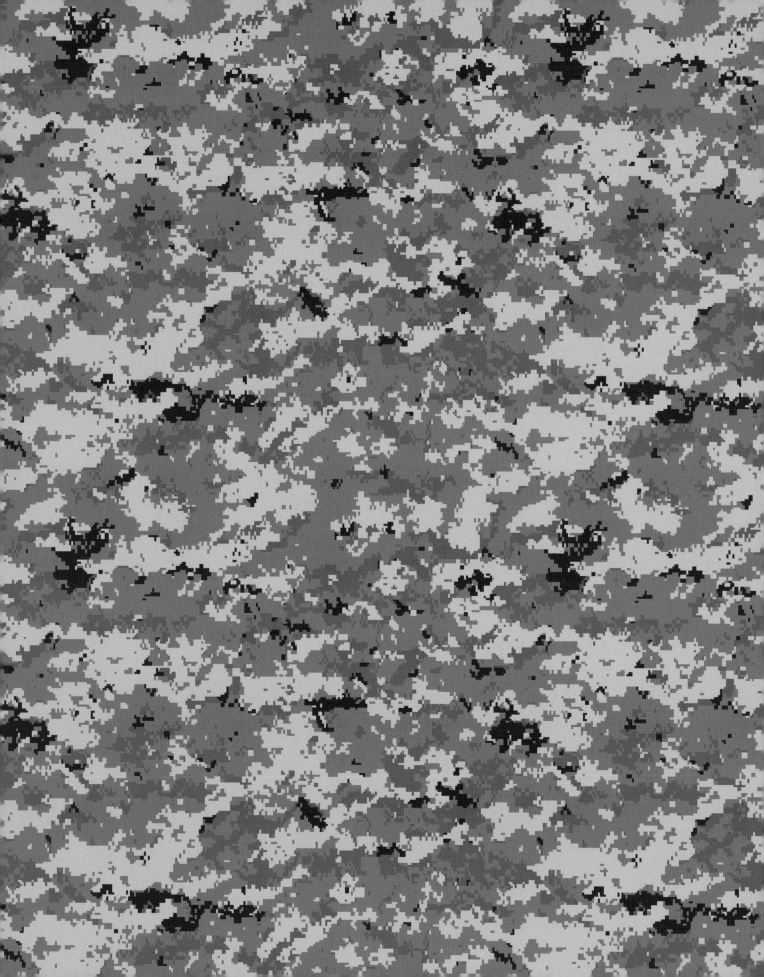

U.S. SPECIAL FORCES

GLOSSARY

covert – hidden, secret

deposed – removed from power

enlisted men – those who sign up voluntarily for military duty at a rank below an officer; they compose the largest part of military units

exfiltrating – removing military units from enemy territory by means of stealth

fatigues – clothing worn by military personnel for duty in the field or while doing manual labor

foregrip – the handle of a weapon mounted under the front part of the barrel

improvised – produced without advance preparation from available materials

intelligence – information about movements and strength of forces of an enemy

Joint Chiefs of Staff – the U.S. president's principal military advisory group, composed of the chiefs of the army, navy, and air force, and the Marine Corps commandant

Monday-morning quarterbacks – people who criticize the decisions of others after the fact

mystique – an aura of mystery and power surrounding something or someone

polymer – a form of plastic noted for its exceptional strength

propaganda – information, especially biased or misleading, that is used to promote a cause or system of beliefs

pseudonym – a fictitious name used by an author to conceal his or her true identity

rucksack – a type of backpack made of strong, waterproof material and often associated with the military

scapegoat – someone singled out for blame of the failure of an operation conducted by an entire group

shoot house – a structure designed to resemble the interior of a house or other building; walls can be moved to create a variety of layouts

squad automatic weapons – lightweight machine guns offering a portable source of automatic weaponry to a small unit

tour of duty – a specific period of time spent in military service

FORCE FACTS Delta Force rescued reported CIA operative Kurt Muse from a notorious Panamanian prison as part of Operation Acid Gambit during the U.S. invasion of Panama in December 1989.

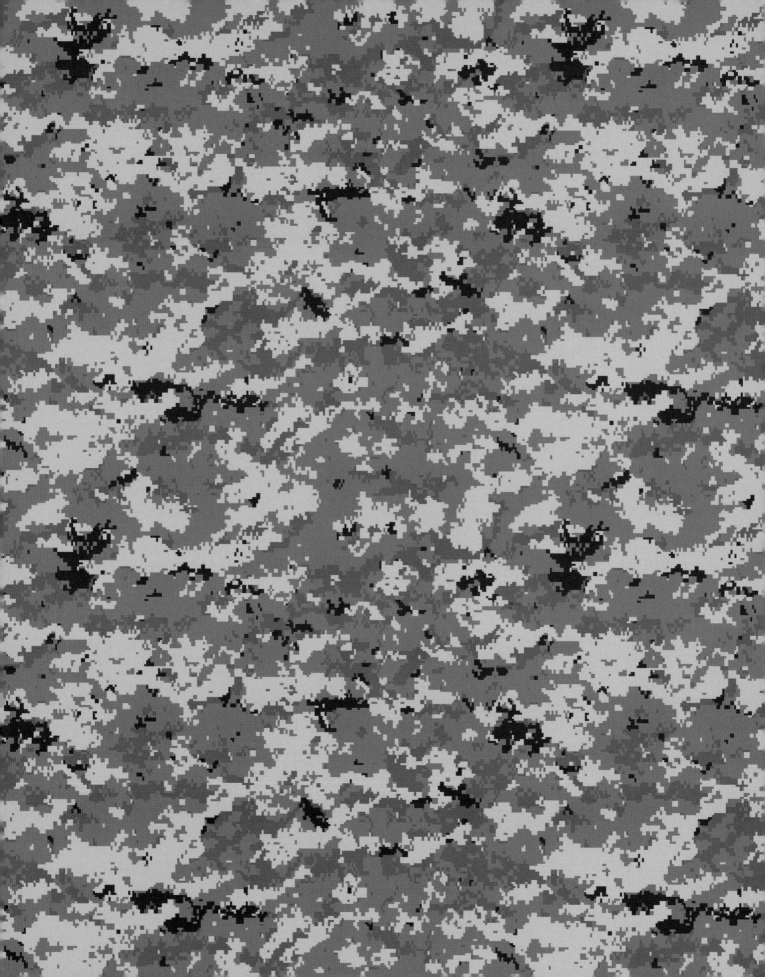

SELECTED BIBLIOGRAPHY

U.S. SPECIAL FORCES

Beckwith, Charlie. *Delta Force: The Army's Elite Counterterrorist Unit*. New York: Avon Books, 2000.

Bowden, Mark. *Black Hawk Down*. New York: Atlantic Monthly Press, 1999.

Chant, Chris. *Special Forces*. Bath, UK: Parragon Books, 2012.

Frederick, Jim. *Special Ops: The Hidden World of America's Toughest Warriors*. New York: Time Books, 2011.

Fury, Dalton. *Kill Bin Laden: A Delta Force Commander's Account of the Hunt for the World's Most Wanted Man*. New York: St. Martin's Press, 2008.

Haney, Eric. *Inside Delta Force: The Story of America's Elite Counterterrorist Unit*. New York: Delacorte Press, 2002.

Lawrence, Richard Russell. *The Mammoth Book of Special Ops*. Philadelphia: Running Press, 2006.

Pushies, Fred. *Weapons of Delta Force*. Minneapolis: Zenith Press, 2010.

WEBSITES

CAG/Delta Force

http://sofrep.com/cag-delta-force/

The Special Operations Forces Situation Report (SOFREP) focuses on the recent history of Delta Force.

How Delta Force Works

http://www.howstuffworks.com/delta-force.htm

This website discusses the structure, weapons, history, and operations of Delta Force and provides a variety of links.

READ MORE

Brush, Jim. *Special Forces*. Mankato, Minn.: Sea-to-Sea, 2012.

Cooper, Jason. *U.S. Special Operations*. Vero Beach, Fla.: Rourke, 2004.

INDEX